An Asperger's Guide To Dating Neurotypicals:
P.S. It's For Married Couples Too

J.R. Reed

ISBN: 10: 1986741796
ISBN-13: 978-1986741798

DEDICATION

First, to my mom and brother, who don't understand my Asperger's, but who love, accept and support me and always have. To my daughter in college, Cameron, who, with a bi-polar mom and a dad on the spectrum, has two strikes against her, but who turned out awesome. I'm very proud of you. My dad passed away in 2002, but I know he would be proud of this book. I wish he were here to read it.

Sarah Smith-Frigerio, a fellow writer and former colleague on a now defunct humor site. Your knowledge of the finer points of Word saved my bacon on this project and I'm beyond grateful. You rock!

Finally to Johnny T, a fellow blogger and Leeann, a friend/semi-stalker who have been there since the early days of my blogging, listening to all my complaints and frustrations. I appreciate the support. I know you wanted a novel, but that's coming later. This was more important.

CONTENTS

FOREWORD

Change is inescapable. Change is also what we fear most, avoid most, and worry about most. But change is so expected that a part of us inevitably retreats into a shell-shocked corner at the very idea. We may come out only when poked (or if there is food). And we await the next vaunted series of changes with grim suspicion coupled with eagerness for the next and newest smartphone.

Thus, I believe the next revolution is not tech but social. It is a revolution hinged upon social currency—our ability to connect, to relate, and to understand. How well will we fare in this process? Will we remain holed up in our little corners of the internet? Or will we break out, using whatever technologies are at hand, to make a name for ourselves by better communicating and being communicated to?

Will we build *community*?

JR's book, *An Asperger's Guide to Dating Neurotypicals*, is a brave and effective jump into this new world of improved social communication and currency. If you are an adult on the spectrum, guess what? You are not alone. You are not broken. And you can be understood and loved. Read this book. Then give it to your partner.

If you are a neurotypical, read this book. JR's real-world writing and personal understanding of autism will open your eyes to the journey that "Aspies" make every day in navigating a world curated by neurotypicals whose brains function much differently than those who are on the spectrum.

No matter how our brains are hardwired, change is hard. Being understood and understanding others? That's what makes this world a little better. And warmer. And more fulfilling.

Joshua Heston, editor-in-chieftain, StateoftheOzarks.net

PREFACE

When I told people this book was being published, the first question I was asked was, "Is it from a straight perspective?" That's an excellent question and as I'm straight and also the one writing the book, I guess the correct answer would be *Yes*.

However, the principles discussed here are based on communication, trust, honesty and sharing. Those traits don't know the difference between straight and LGB, so the real answer to the question is *No*. This book is written from the perspective of a straight guy who wants couples to succeed whether they are the same or opposite sex.

Also, there is no set age range for the reader of this book. With the exception of the chapter on sex, I would say it's for everyone from high school on up. I have my opinion and belief when it comes to sex among those in high school but I'm not forcing those beliefs on anyone. What you do is your own choice.

The principles in this book aren't revolutionary or groundbreaking but they are solid, time-tested and laid out in an easy-to-read way using analogies that are easy to understand and not using clinical terms that need to be looked up.

It's my hope that in reading this book those who are in good relationships will now have great relationships and those who are in bad relationships will be able to repair their relationships (if indeed the pairing of the two of you is right). If you can't repair the relationship, my hope is that you realize it before any emotional or physical damage is done and that you can part on amicable terms.

For those not currently in a relationship, I want you to be able to go into your next relationship with the tools you need to make it work for you. Remember that having the tools is only half the job. Knowing the proper way to use the tools is what really counts.

I'm a firm believer that not every relationship is meant to work out, but if you apply the principles laid out here (and things go south) you can still walk away with your head held high and know you did everything you could to make it work and there is absolutely no shame in that!

Research is constantly being done regarding autism and its causes. One organization (which shall remain nameless) sought a cure for autism for many years. The problem is that we don't need to be cured because there's nothing wrong with us!

Neurodivergence and neurodiversity are two of the newer terms being used in the autism field and, though there are many definitions you'll find floating around out there, what they really mean is this:

Neurodivergent is the atypical neurological brain, also knows as the autistic brain. That's where we get the term neurotypical (or NT) for those not on the spectrum.

Neurodiversity is a concept where the neurological differences among us are recognized and accepted. It's recognizing that those on the spectrum don't need to be cured but rather need to be accepted and integrated into mainstream society simply as people.

I would take it one step further and say that a mixture of those with autism and those without make for a great team because many Aspies are out-of-the-box thinkers and look at things in a different light than our NT brothers and sisters do.

Put neurotypicals and neurodivergents together in a relationship, social group, or in the workplace, and suddenly you have a different and amazing dynamic. I bring this up now because it's a concept that will be mentioned throughout the book.

I want to thank Dr. Linda Barboa, Jan Luck and Elizabeth Obrey (of Stars For Autism) for their support as I wrote this book as well as Joshua Heston and Dale Grubaugh (of State of the Ozarks Creative Community) for their friendship and help when I moved 1,800 miles away and knew no one. I couldn't have done this without you all.

Last, but not least, I want to give a shout-out to my wingman, Tye, my black lab autism service dog. So far he hasn't scored me any dates, but I'm optimistic in his skills.

Being that I'm on the spectrum, it's possible that he's gotten a few girls to flirt with me, but as Aspies aren't always great at picking up on cues like that, I may have missed out on some golden opportunities. I need to teach him to bite me in the butt when he's working for me and I'm missing the signs!

Enjoy the book and I hope it helps in ways you never imagined. Please leave comments regarding this book at www.purplechin.com or at Amazon.

Ch.1 Explaining the Differences Between Us

Let me get a couple housekeeping issues out of the way first. The term Asperger's refers to someone who is high functioning autistic. In 2013, the terms *Asperger's, high-functioning autistic*, and *autism* were "officially" dropped and replaced by simply saying that people are "on the spectrum."

The reality is that professionals still use all the above words when describing us. I say us because I'm proudly Asperger's. It's my superpower.

When I use the term Asperger's, autistic, autism, or spectrum, I mean the same thing. To me (and to most in the field) those words are interchangeable. I also use the word Aspie which is a shortened, and politically correct term to describe someone with Asperger's.

Also, this book isn't written toward any one sexual orientation. The principles I discuss are universal to all types of relationships and that's because the principles are based on communication, honesty, trust, openness and understanding. Those principles don't care about the difference of genders involved in the relationship, and quite frankly, as long as you find that this book helps your relationship, neither do I.

The differences in our relationships have to do with our attitudes and our way of looking at— and treating—our partner and not our sexuality. So for the purposes of this book when I use the terms, "Relationship" or, "Partner," I mean both LGB and straight. I know this will offend some but I ask that you look at this book for what it truly is—a guide to dating, marriage and relationships and not a guide to gender-specific relationships.

The word *Crazy* is a broad term and one, which I think, is used in the wrong context more than it is in the correct one. As a society, anyone who is different is deemed crazy but I'm using it here in a slightly different context:

Everyone, whether NT or Aspie, has their quirks, idiosyncrasies and things that are distinctly their own form of crazy. The idea behind finding an ideal partner is finding someone who can handle your individual brand of crazy while you are handling his or her unique kind of crazy.

I use the word as a general term and it's really focused more on the traits of the person and not their mental state of being.

Using myself as an example: I'm not OCD but I can't stand clutter. That doesn't mean that things don't get cluttered up from time to time, but when they do, I'm overly stressed and make it a point to clean it up ASAP. So a slob would not be my type of crazy.

I also have a need to be on time and cannot stand being late. That's one thing that contributed to the demise of my last relationship. Lilly (not her real name) lived about forty-five minutes away and there were several times when, say, at 7:00 p.m., she would text and say, "I'm getting in my car right now." Then at 8:00 she would call and say she was now leaving!

At 8:30 I would call her and find that she was only five minutes from home. That bothered me like you can't believe, but to her it was just life as usual and she couldn't understand why it bothered me.

I asked a lot of questions (mostly for clarification of things she said). As you get further into this book, you'll see that this is an important part of the communication process—making sure that you fully understand what the other person is saying. Lilly got frustrated with that and that's one example of how she couldn't handle my type of crazy. Remember the made up name Lilly, as she will be used again later in the book.

This is what I mean by finding a partner where you can both handle their type of crazy. No one needs to get locked up for a 72-hour evaluation. You just need to be able to accept and handle the things that make your partner, or potential partner, unique.

A question that often comes up is, "When do I tell the NT person I'm dating—or want to date— that I'm on the spectrum?"

That's a really good question without a simple answer. The easiest answer is this: When you feel comfortable telling them and feel like they will accept you for who you are as an Aspie.

Another answer is: Sooner rather than later. It's my personal belief that the longer you wait to tell them, the more it looks like you're hiding something and that you're trying to get them to fall in love—or at least deep in like—with you and then you're going to spring it on them.

In my case, I really don't have to worry, as I have my autism service dog. Tye is a black lab mix that goes with me everywhere. Before the first date I have to prepare her for the fact that we're going to have a four-legged chaperone.

The bottom line is that the NT may need a little teaching as to what Asperger's is all about. I've found that the general population has no clue what we're really like and what Asperger's entails. But, once they know, often times it's not as big a deal as they—or you— may have originally thought. If it's going to be a deal breaker with them, wouldn't you rather know early on before you get too invested with the relationship? I can't speak for you, but I know I would.

Now, let's delve into what makes the NT and the Aspie different. Sure, we all know that our brains are wired differently but that doesn't make one type of brain better than the other. An Asperger's brain simply processes things differently than the brain of a neurotypical.

Here's an example:

My younger brother—three years younger—is a NT and when we talk about ideas or projects, my brain goes into what I call Aspie mode. That means my brain starts running every possible scenario that I can picture and viewing the outcome.

I can't necessarily see the details and steps taken along the way but I can quickly see if any given scenario is likely to work or not. When I tell him that I don't think it will work the way he's thinking of doing it, he tells me that I'm being negative, and frankly, that hurts a lot. I'm not being negative. I'm being realistic. Sometimes I'm given the opportunity to share a different way to try whatever it is we're talking about and sometimes I'm not.

That's how the Aspie brain works. We see things and figure out the optimal solution to the problem at hand, or at least try to. In a relationship it's not always the best way to go about things and with the principles I talk about in later chapters, this can be dealt with in a way that makes the Aspie feel like they're not having to change who they are and the NT doesn't feel like the Aspie is attempting to be smarter than they are and has all the answers,

Which leads me straight into a myth I want to bust. Raise your hand if you've heard or if you believe that the Asperger's brain is better or smarter than the brain of a neurotypical. *Please keep your hands held high for a few minutes so I can get a count.* Also, if you're reading this late at night, you may have to keep it up for a while because chances are I'm asleep and won't see it until I get up.

Many people from both Asperger's and NT communities believe that the Asperger's brain functions on a higher level than the NT brain and that's simply not true. Our brains are wired *differently*. It is a different way of thinking. A different way from getting from Point A to Point B.

The only thing I know about electricity is that when I flip the switch, something is supposed to turn on. If it doesn't and it's more than changing a light bulb, I'm stuck. Thus, I turned to two friends from my Facebook Asperger's Life Support group for the following analogy.

If you're a loving NT of an Aspie (or if you're on the spectrum) I encourage you to go to Facebook and search Asperger's Life Support. Chris Godley does a great job with all of us. But back to the analogy.

I asked a couple of people in the group with electrical backgrounds for examples of how to best explain this to you and I was told that it's like a string of Christmas lights. Some run on a series circuit and some on a parallel circuit. When plugged in, both types of circuits light up with festive holiday cheer, but if you have a bulb burn out, one type of circuit shuts down all the lights where the other type keeps the other bulbs lit.

If that doesn't make sense, another explained it like AC vs. DC current. Both will power things but DC (Direct Current) only flows one way while AC (Alternating Current) can be reversed, sending flow both ways. One isn't better than the other. It just depends on what you need to power.

Besides the way the brain works, the Aspie will have one or more of the traits listed below. Not every person on the spectrum is the same and there are situations that some can handle quite easily where others would be shaking in the corner at the same situation.

I was diagnosed late in life, at age forty-six, because I was well out of high school before autism was recognized in the classroom and before Asperger's was even a term. I won't bore you with the long story because you can read all about it at www.notweirdjustautistic.com.

The bottom line is that for forty-six years I was teased and mocked by teachers, students and employers—even being called Forrest, as in Gump, by one employer for four years—and I had to find ways to cope with each of these situations. I eventually learned what triggered certain reactions. At the time, I called them "Weird episodes" in my life, so I learned to avoid them. It's important that you learn your triggers and sometimes the best person for that job is your significant other as they are around you more than others, they care, and they have a vested interest in you.

All Aspies have triggers (things that set us off) of some kind but we don't all have the same triggers. There are a lot of common triggers and we'll discuss those in the next chapter.

In society we generally refer to this as *pushing their buttons* and that's a good way of looking at it as well though I draw a distinction between pushing buttons and pulling the trigger on an Aspie. In my eyes, a person on the spectrum has triggers that set them off and the NT has buttons that can be pushed by the Aspie. It's not right to do either one of those things but, sadly, it happens all the time in relationships.

Once we get triggered we tend to go into Meltdown Mode. Most people can't tell a *meltdown* from a *tantrum* but there is a huge difference.

When someone, usually a child, throws a tantrum it's because they want something and they have an audience to perform for. Take away the audience and you generally take away the tantrum.

When someone on the spectrum has a meltdown, it's because one of his or her triggers has been, well, triggered. It doesn't matter if they're in a house alone or in a football stadium with 90,000 people, that meltdown is going to happen until the Aspie feels comfortable again and whatever triggered the meltdown has stopped or gone away.

Simply put, a meltdown is an intense response to an overwhelming situation and we, for a period of time, lose control of our behavior. It's not something we're proud of and generally the only way to avoid a meltdown is to avoid interacting with people or simply avoiding situations that we know will put us in a panicked mode (much like the Thanksgiving episode that we'll talk about in the next chapter).

Your partner's trigger's are important for the NT in a relationship to know because often times we'll get accused of being a baby or having a tantrum when we don't get our way and that's just not true. We've just been triggered, much like a bomb, and we went off.

In a good relationship the NT will use their knowledge of the Aspies' triggers for good and in a bad relationship they will use the triggers for evil— and keep pulling the trigger until the partner melts down. That's what we (as advocates) term, "Not cool." I know that doesn't sound like a clinical term but I'm an advocate and not a clinician. And really that's what it is: a way for one person to screw with another simply for their own entertainment. I've dated a couple women who used their power for evil and I had a special word for them, which I choose not to share here!

To keep it fair, although I don't recall ever purposely pushing the buttons of someone I've dated just for fun, I'm sure there have been occasions where I've pushed their buttons without thinking about what I was doing or about their feelings and, while maybe not quite as bad as doing it intentionally, it still doesn't excuse my actions.

Keep in mind that I'm not bagging on women. It can be men pulling the trigger on their female Aspie partners as well. It's just that I'm a guy and the analogies that immediately pop into my head are of women doing rotten things to men. I'll be the first to admit that we can be just as cruel as our female counterparts and it doesn't matter who pulls the trigger. This type of gun should always be set on safety.

Just as I'm asking NT's to not set off the triggers of their partners on the spectrum, the same goes for us Aspies as well. Don't knowingly push the buttons of your partners because you want to get back at them or for any other reason. Being cruel is being cruel, no matter how you look at it.

Here are a few of the common traits we Aspies have:

Fear and avoidance of social situations, even simple ones
Self-esteem issues and self-doubt
Sensory overload—the things around us easily over-stimulate us
Panic attacks and anxiety
Depression
Difficulties with social interactions including recognizing facial expressions, tone of voice, jokes, sarcasm and social rules that NT's would consider unwritten.
Engaging in repetitive behaviors. Remember this one when we get to the chapter on sex.

This is not remotely an exhaustive list as there are plenty of books available on the general subject of spectrum disorders (and all the possible signs and effects caused by it). They are, however, the more common ones and enough for us and for the subject that we're talking about—relationships.

As you read further into this book remember that the basic principles that will help you form an amazing relationship are simple principles but ones we often forget about in the heat of the moment. They are communication, respect, understanding, honesty, and sharing. These are all things that are important to a relationship between two NT's, but are crucial in the success of a relationship with an Aspie.

Remember that as much an as Aspie wants to control some of their traits, often times it's just not possible and the NT will decide if that's something they can deal with. Likewise with the NT's. They may not want to change some of their unique traits (and that's OK), but the Aspie has to decide if that's something they want to live with.

The good news is that great relationships are possible and though it takes some work it's not a huge undertaking. Let's move on to the next chapter where we will talk a bit more about the common traits just mentioned and a few of the more common triggers.

Ch. 2 More On the Common Traits and Triggers

As promised just a page ago, here is a discussion of some of the common traits that people with Asperger's have (along with many of the overlapping triggers). Please remember that the list of traits and triggers is long and any given Aspie (hopefully) only has a handful of them. Some of these are on my personal list:

Fear and avoidance of social situations—For many years I coached youth ice hockey with kids age eight through high school varsity. This means I had to interact with a new group of players and parents each season. Each season I put on a brave face, introduced myself and began working with the kids on the ice and interacting with the parents off the ice.

For me it was much easier to work with the kids on the ice as we were skating and doing different drills but the older the kids got, the more fearful I became of being on the ice with them.

When I was thirty-nine I had a stroke and it took away a lot of the hockey abilities I had before. Coaching kids who were flat-out better players than me intimidated me like you can't believe.

I know it sounds stupid to be afraid of being on the ice with sixteen- to eighteen-year-olds, but it was and it also caused a lot of self-esteem issues (which is the next trait).

It wasn't the players that I was most frightened of; it was the parents. I felt socially awkward around them. In a group setting it wasn't as bad, though I still had to overcome a lot of fear. One-on-one interaction and small groups were the worst because, like most people on the spectrum, I'm not always sure when a conversation is over or when it should be over. I always know when I want it to be over (and that's as soon as it starts).

There were certain players I had for several years in a row, so having the same parents over and over made it a bit easier, but as much as I tried to put on a brave face, as soon as I hit my car, the panic attack I had been holding in was generally released and would last for hours.

In these social situations, our partners can help take some of the load off, even by just being there. Knowing that there was someone by my side who loved me and had my back would have made all the difference in the world. It wouldn't have taken away the attacks completely but it would have made them more manageable.

Self-esteem issues and self doubt—When you go through the first forty-six years of your life not knowing you're autistic—but knowing something is "wrong" with you—self-esteem issues are going to pop up. Add in the ridicule and harassment I endured as well as the constant reminders that I wasn't living up to my potential and you can see why I constantly doubted my ability to do anything.

As far back as high school I wanted to write, but my high school journalism teacher, on more than one occasion, suggested I drop the class and take something else because I "couldn't write and never would." It took me fifteen years before I got the courage to take a junior college journalism class and then do some freelance work for a local bi-weekly newspaper. That class and bi-weekly paper jump-started a career that's lasted more than twenty years and has landed me articles in more than thirty different magazines and a dozen newspapers. I've been lucky enough to cover two Stanley Cup Finals, dozens of NASCAR races and interviewed celebrities like Penn & Teller, John O' Hurley, Wayne Gretzky and others. You would think with that resume, I would be on top of the world, but I still have my self-doubts. Why? Because I'm an Aspie and that's just how we roll.

Sensory overload—We are easily over stimulated by the things around us and have to be careful about what we do and where we go. We need to learn to pace ourselves. That doesn't mean that we become the party poopers, it just means that we have to allow ourselves some downtime throughout the week or weekend to let our brains re-boot, recharge and get ready for the next adventure.

If we get overloaded, it's either major meltdown time or we sleep for hours on end. And by hours, I mean twelve to fifteen hours at a stretch with a few periods of wakefulness and then back to bed for more recharging. Sensory overload is not pretty and something I really struggled with before my diagnosis. At the time I couldn't figure out why I couldn't go out and do all the same things my friends were doing.

Once our partners are aware of what overloads our brain, they can help guide us and remind us that doing _____ may not be such a good idea considering all the other things we've done and that maybe it's time for a break. That doesn't mean they become our mom or dad but rather our best friend who is looking out for our best interest.

Panic attacks and anxiety—Any of our fears or triggers can set these off quickly and they can last for fifteen minutes or they can last for hours. Honestly, there's no telling how long one will last and they can all be different.

If our NT partners can see things coming that they know will trigger a panic attack or anxiety in us, maybe they can step in and smooth the situation out and, in a sense, advocate for us.

I had a panic attack today as I had to stop in to see my psychiatrist's nurse because he accidentally wrote the wrong dosage for a prescription that somehow got called into a mail order pharmacy that delivered a three-month supply of medicine with a dose way too low.

There's nothing wrong with the nurse, but it's a large, busy practice and I was dropping in unannounced. I didn't know how anyone would react, how long I would have to wait to see her and for some reason, I felt like it was partially my fault, even though I knew for a fact I had done nothing wrong.

Depression—There's not a lot to say about this one, as it's pretty self-explanatory and is very common among those on the spectrum. The littlest things can get us depressed and that's why it's crucial that we continue to see our psychiatrists on a regular basis and take our medications as prescribed. If we see a psychologist, don't hold back. Let it all out and your chances of feeling better increase dramatically. Take it from a guy who spent many years telling his psychologist that everything was fine, when in reality, everything was a living nightmare. These doctors and therapists are there for a reason. Use them to their full potential.

Difficulties with social interactions include recognizing facial expressions, tone of voice, jokes, sarcasm and social rules that NT's would consider unwritten. We've already covered the basics of social interaction a few paragraphs ago but understanding how someone is saying something or how they mean something can be very difficult for us. Someone can say something totally innocent and mean nothing by it but because we can't properly read their expression or tone of voice, we think they're making fun of us. The key word in that last sentence is *think*. They may not be mocking us but we go off for no reason because we think they are.

It can also go the other way and someone may be ripping us apart and making fun of us directly to our faces without us being the slightest bit aware of what's happening. I'm sure that's happened to every Aspie at some point in their life, more likely in their early years.

Having a partner who can translate for us is a blessing like you can't believe. If you've every watched the TV show *Scorpion* you know what I mean. The premise of the show is of a team of geniuses who are government contractors. Since they're all high IQ'd (and presumably autistic) they need someone to translate the world for them and run interference on their behalf. In the case of the show, it's a woman named Paige who has a young son with a genius IQ. The geniuses translate Paige's son for her and she translates the clients for them. It's a win-win. I truly believe that all Aspies needs a Paige in their life.

Engaging in repetitive behaviors—We all have our things that we like and that make us feel comfortable. Routines are uber important for us. Get us out of our routine and a panic attack usually isn't far behind. Everyone on the spectrum is different when it comes to their repetitive behavior but it's generally something we can't control and often times something we don't even realize we're doing.

When I'm deep in thought, concentrating on something or working hard, I tend to stick the tip of my tongue out of my mouth. I actually just paused as I'm writing this and, yes, my tongue was out there. I made a conscious effort to put my tongue back, but my guess is by the time I start the next paragraph, it will be back out. *Nope. It's already back out.*

Our NT partners are going to have to get used to these repetitive behaviors because, as mentioned before, they're typically not something that can be changed or that will just disappear. The NT has to decide if they can live with the repetitive behavior or if they need to just cut and run. If the latter is the case, I strongly suggest for the Aspie's sake that you do it sooner rather than later.

Remember our talk on repetitive behavior when we get to the chapter on sex.

Triggers:
Sensory overload—crowds, loud noise or certain noise such as fireworks, bright lights, strobe lights, certain smells, especially foods and cleaning products

Unstructured time—structure is important because with unstructured time we don't know what we should be doing and then we panic.

Public speaking or in-class/work presentations

Changes in plans—again, structure is important

Being around young kids—they're unpredictable, they're loud and did I mention, very unpredictable

Concerts—loud noises coupled with large crowds

Social situations such as having conversations—we don't know exactly what to say or when to end a conversation and thus we feel uncomfortable

Let me give you a prime example of a couple triggers of mine and why having the NT respect the Aspie in these situations is very important. I call it "The Great Thanksgiving Fiasco of 2017" and it goes like this:

I started dating Lilly (again, not her real name) in October of 2017 and the first date was great, as was the second, third, fourth and probably even the fifth. Things were humming along nicely until shortly before Thanksgiving when Lilly invited me to go with her to her hometown to enjoy the holiday with her family.

Ask an Aspie what it's like to be in a closed setting with a lot of people you don't know and they will tell you it's terrifying. I knew from past family holiday gatherings of my own (where I knew everyone or almost everyone) that it would be a very difficult experience for me and that's why I told Lilly several times, even as recent as the night before Thanksgiving, that I preferred staying home with Tye and just cooking a chicken by myself.

I knew how badly she wanted me to go and meet her family and I knew that she had prepared her family for the fact that the guy she was dating was autistic and had a service dog. Just the mere thought of meeting all these people and having to talk to some of them freaked me out like you can't believe.

To say she wasn't happy that I was considering staying home is a huge understatement and so I did what any good/stupid Aspie boyfriend would do. I sucked it up, brought a couple extra anxiety pills and went with her. Big mistake!

It was everything I expected and more. We came in the back door and I planted myself in a chair and didn't get up out of that chair until it was time to eat. Lilly asked me several times to come mingle and every time I said no, I could see her frustration growing.

Sorry, but if I didn't want to be there in the first place, there was no way I was going into the kitchen and the main part of the house because that's where most people were and so at mealtime, Lilly fixed me a plate and brought it to the table I moved to, a mere eight feet from where I had been sitting the past few hours, mostly alone, while she hung with her family.

After dinner, the room I was in started filling up and I began to panic. I took Tye out for a short walk and when I came back inside, there were even more people in the room and the panic attack went from Code Orange to a full-on Code Blue. I told Lilly I was going out to the car and would not be coming back in. I was trying to be polite and told her she could come out whenever she wanted to, but the reality was that I wanted to get the heck out of Dodge ASAP (not the real name of her hometown).

"Whenever she wanted to," turned into more than an hour while I sat in a freezing car and fumed that the woman I was dating didn't care that I was having a major panic attack. After a half dozen texts from her, bordering on "demanding" that I come in (and me responding that I was staying put because of the panic attack) she finally took the clue that I wasn't coming back in and stopped texting (though she stayed inside with her family a while longer).

When she finally arrived at my car, she told me that her family wasn't happy that I didn't come in to say goodbye. She also informed me that she told her family I had stomach issues and that's why I was in the car.

I was upset that she hadn't been honest and didn't tell them I was having a panic attack. In my mind, she was embarrassed about me and that's what started the off-again portion of our on- again/off-again relationship.

Again, I'm not saying this to make her feel bad but it genuinely hurt that the woman I was dating was ashamed of who I really was and couldn't share that with her family.

Also, I was hurt that she was really upset at me for having the huge panic attack I had warned her about for weeks and which could have been avoided if only I stayed home. She didn't realize, though I voiced it several times, that reminding me how upset she was that I didn't come back in wasn't making the panic attack go away any faster.

That three-hour drive back home was extremely awkward. I was literally shaking and she couldn't understand why. After a couple weeks, we talked (though she still couldn't figure out why it was wrong to not tell her family the truth) and we tried dating again. This time I think it probably lasted all of a weekend.

It didn't matter how many times we talked about communication, there never seemed to be much of our interaction that went right. I could go on and on for hours but the bottom line is that our relationship would all turn into a disaster within forty-eight hours of trying again.

I liken a romantic relationship to driving down the same road every day. A road that the city needs to fix in a big way! It's a road is full of potholes and you can either hit them every day and throw your car and your back out of alignment, or you can learn where the potholes are and navigate your way around them so you have a smooth commute.

We tried to navigate the potholes a few times, but nothing ever seemed to work for more than a few days at a time. Communication between us was horrible, though as mentioned before, we talked a strong communication strategy, and once the communication broke down, so did everything else.

Lilly lives about forty-five minutes away with roommates and I live alone with Tye, so most weekends she would come down to my log cabin near the lakes on Friday night. There were times that by Saturday night I was ready to have her pack up and head home. But I rarely said anything because of the extra drama I knew that would ensue. Does that make me a wimp? Probably, and I own that, though not proudly.

The funny thing is that in early March of 2018 I wrote a blog post about this Thanksgiving incident at www.notweirdjustautistic.com and in the blog post I wrote the following three paragraphs. Less than a week later, I began writing this book.

"I could go on and on for many chapters and possibly even a book on this subject, but the last big tip to leave you with today is to develop a respect for each other and the differences between the two of you. The reality is that the Aspie has certain limitations, many of which are social, and the NT partner needs to be ready, willing and able to pick up the slack and lift the other up.

Just as autistic kids have meltdowns, so do adults. If we allow ourselves to get over- stimulated, more often than not things go south quickly. I know my limitations as far as stimulation and sensory overload go, and my partner, if indeed I ever decide to date again (and right now that's a HUGE if), needs to know as well and needs to be able to see the warning signs.

If our partners know our triggers and can help us manage them, that is more of a blessing than an NT could ever imagine."

Ch. 3 Neurodivergent and Neurodiveraity

Neurodivergent. It sounds like the fourth movie in an already-finished trilogy. Now that I think about it, I wonder what it would take to get the rights to make a fourth film based on the same characters. I know a blogger who writes exclusively on being Neurodivergent (and the subject of neurodiversity) and I know together we could write an amazing script. I'll have to put that project on the back burner until after this book is finished.

If you've read this far into the book and have accepted what I've written so far, then congratulations, you are a believer in being Neurodivergent and in neurodiversity. We've briefly touched on the topics already but let's get into what they really mean and how they fit into the Aspie & NT relationship.

Neurodivergent is a young term in the fields of psychology and autism and simply put it means that someone has a brain that significantly diverges from the societal norm. It's not limited to autism. It could be dyslexia or it could be from a horrific automobile accident. It just means different and different does NOT mean bad or broken.

Neurodiversity is the diversity of the human brain. Just by picking up this book you've accepted that the brain of one partner looks at things differently than the brain of the other partner. Neither is better or worse, just different and it's in accepting, celebrating and finding ways for those two brains to not only co-exist but to thrive and take the relationship to new levels that makes neurodiversity such an awesome thing.

Both these terms are hip and trendy right now and though I would identify myself more as a middle-aged hipster with a purple goatee, *hip and trendy* are not two words I would use to describe myself. I'm more old school, though I do believe in Neurodivergence and neurodiversity with every fiber of my being.

Aspies, as discussed earlier, are out-of-the box thinkers. We see a problem, situation or actually anything, and go into what I call Aspie mode. This is where our brains start running scenarios at about 90 miles an hour, throwing out the ones that won't work and keeping the ones that will. When we don't easily find workable solutions, we think outside the box until we find the one that will work the best.

It sounds difficult, and it is to some point, though not nearly as difficult as convincing our NT partners that the out-of-the box ideas we have are not completely insane. That's where communication comes in and that's in the next chapter, so hang on and stick with me for a few pages more. This chapter will be fairly short.

There are some who think those on the spectrum need to be fixed. If we're not broken, why do we need to be fixed? In fact, until last year one of the leading autism organizations in the world took a majority of their donation money and put it towards finding a cure for autism. Autism isn't a disease, so why does it need a cure? It doesn't.

Spend your money to find a cure for cancer or Alzheimers and let us on the spectrum be proud of who we are and not be made to feel ashamed because we're "sick." I'm not sick. Are any other Aspies out there sick because of their autism? I didn't think so.

At the time, this same organization had no people on the board who were autistic. Now they have four. Out of twenty-four board members they have *four.* I'm not sure whom this group thinks they speak for, but they certainly don't speak for me.

I apologize for the mini-rant. Back to neurodiversity. We're talking about dating and relationships, but neurodiversity can be applied to any social situation whether it is school, work, church, a charitable or social group.

I'm a nerd, but I'm definitely not a Trekkie, although watching William Shatner "act" is pretty funny. I've also watched a little *Star Trek: The Next Generation.* In Next Generation, the Borg wanted to assimilate everyone into their civilization—or as they called it, a collective. Their minds were linked together in something called "the Hive." Again, I'm NOT a Trekkie. I used Wikipedia to get this info.

There are some who think we're broken and want to assimilate us and find ways to change us so that we fit societal norms. Why would anyone want to do that? If that were the case and everyone fit a certain societal mold, we'd be nothing more than clones or, as stated before, "Borg in a hive-like collective."

I don't know about you, but I like being me and I like dating someone who's her own person. If we were all the same, not only would that be uber-creepy, but also it would get very boring, very fast.

Just as we have different ethnicities, sexes, religions and backgrounds, so are we neurodiverse.

Here's a funny story. The other day I had to fill out a form and for the life of me I could not figure out why they needed my ethnicity. I looked down at the usual ones: African-American, American Indian, Pacific Islander, Asian, Caucasian, and so on. At the end it said, "Other" and had a line below it to fill in what the other was. I checked, "Other" and wrote, "Neurodiverse." I really wish I could be there when the person looked at the form and tried to figure out what that meant!

Aspies, be proud that you're Neurodivergent, not ashamed of it! I'm a proud Aspie and I don't mind telling people that I'm autistic. Just as we shouldn't be ashamed of it, our NT partners should be proud of who we are and shouldn't be ashamed to tell people that their partner is on the spectrum.

Too many people think they know all about autism because they watched *Rain Man*. Now, Dustin Hoffman played an amazing character in that movie, but the character is not what you would call a high-functioning autistic. Hoffman's character is an autistic savant and a savant is very low functioning as far as the autism side of the brain goes, but amazingly gifted (generally in mathematical calculations or music).

Too many people—when they hear someone is dating an autistic person—immediately picture a guy in a light-colored suit rattling on and on about Wapner and what time he's on.

If that's what many think of people on the spectrum, then it's no wonder our partners are often afraid or ashamed to identify us as Aspies to their friends, family or colleagues. This is where public education comes in and that's something that I'm very passionate about. Hopefully we can teach others who we really are and that we're not some lame stereotype.

The more I think about it, the more I realize just how much I really dislike using the words, "Us, them, we and you." It sounds like I'm looking up at one group and down at another and that's not true. I honestly can't find other words to use in this context, so please know that, as I've said many times already, in my opinion no one brain is better than another, with the possible exception of Albert Einstein and Stephen Hawking, may they both rest in peace.

To sum it up, being Neurodivergent simply means that our brains are different than the accepted norm, and there's nothing wrong with that. Neurodiversity is the celebration that we all have brains that function in different ways and if we can work together and harness that power for good, there's nothing we as a collective society, or in this case as a couple, cannot do.

Now let's move onto effective communication in the Aspie/NT relationship.

Ch. 4 Why Communication is Key

As technology advances, so do the ways we communicate with each other. This is going to make me sound like an old man—though I prefer the term" Middle-aged hipster"—but when I was in high school and college, we had telephones, U.S. mail and face-to-face talking.

There were no fax machines, cell phones, pagers, FaceTime, Skype, text messaging, or e-mail. That can be looked at as both a bad thing and a good thing. Modern technology can be a huge distraction in relationships, but when used correctly, that technology can help people stay close and feel connected, even over great distances.

The key to all the technology we have now (and all that we'll have in the near future) is to use it correctly and at the proper time. The bottom line is that when you're together with your significant other, nothing is worse than having one or both of you with their heads constantly buried in their cell phone or tablet, completely ignoring the other person. And no, texting each other from opposite sides of the couch is NOT good communication.

Sure there will be times when one or both of you is working and have to use their gadgets, but the point I'm trying to get across is that you don't ignore your partner and make them feel less important that Twitter, Facebook, Instagram or whatever else you're doing. If those other things are truly more important than the one you love or like, then you need to let them know so they can hit the road and find someone who will appreciate them and spend time with them.

I'm not proud to admit it, but I've been guilty of burying my face in my phone or tablet and I've also been on the receiving end if it, so I know how much it hurts. That's something I never want to do to anyone again and something I promise the next person I date that I won't do.

Speaking of the next person I date, if indeed I decide to date again, let's talk about the last person I dated. Don't worry ladies, this isn't going to be me bashing her and laying it all at her feet. This is a clear and honest assessment of how a breakdown of communication ended our relationship. Again, let me reiterate that I am not speaking poorly of her, rather explaining why things didn't work between us. She's a great person, just not the right person for me.

First let me give you a brief history.

In August of 2017 I moved from Southern California to the Ozarks, on purpose. Besides fathering my daughter, it was the best thing I've ever done. As you can well imagine for someone with Asperger's, Los Angeles, Long Beach and Orange County can be sensory overload on steroids. On top of that I was an ice hockey coach who took on as many as five teams at a time plus taught private and group lessons.

The noise of the pucks smashing off the boards during practices and lessons was usually too much for me and I would leave the rink and go home to lay down for a bit just to get my wits about me again. When it came to dealing with parents, it was scary. I always had great parents, but still, the social anxiety Aspies feel was overwhelming at times and there were many occasions where I had to excuse myself so I could go to the coaches' locker room just to calm down.

The Ozarks are the opposite. Traffic here is when there are six cars at a stop sign. My home is less than ten minutes away from two lakes and at least two-dozen hiking trails. Compared to where I came from, it's Aspie heaven. Now back to the story.

I arrived in Missouri in August and got Tye, my amazing autism service dog, in early October. He was a shelter dog, just as all dogs from Dog's Nation are. Dog's Nation rescued him when he was about eighteen months old and trained him for two years before handing him off to me. My first date with this girl was also my first date with Tye as my wingman and I was terrified.

In the past I had always wondered when the right time was to tell the person I was dating about my Asperger's. There's no right answer, but I would say early on is best. Otherwise, they may feel like you were hiding something from them and that's never good.

Now with Tye, I had no choice but to be right upfront about my condition. I mean, you don't walk in to a first date with a black lab in a vest saying, "SERVICE DOG," and find a way to hide it.

When we talked on the phone, I told Lilly (not her real name), that I had Asperger's, explained a bit about it, told her not to worry about it, and let her know that Tye would be joining us. To my utter surprise, she was fine with it and we had a few great dates.

As things progressed, we started talking more about our individual needs and expectations. We both agreed that communication was at the top of the list because, even though there had been a few great dates, there had also been a few moments of confusion, frustration and a lack of understanding the needs of each other.

I provided her with information on Asperger's traits and we talked about them, highlighting the ones that were most prevalent in me. One thing to remember about Aspies is that each person doesn't have every trait or trigger; another reason that communication early on about what triggers, "Aspie moments" in us is so important.

Talking about communication and actually communicating are two totally different things. Lilly and I were great at talking about communicating but when it came time to actually communicate, we weren't so great.

She knew that I had a lot of stress in my life, so she didn't want to "burden me" with her problems. Sharing her problems with me wasn't going to be a burden. It was going to allow me to understand her better and to help her, if indeed she wanted my help. Her not sharing also kept things bottled up inside and that's not a good thing for anyone.

Imagine if you will, a can of your favorite soft drink. Shake it up, throw it around, put it through things that will be stressful to the contents inside and then open it up. I don't have to tell you what happens when you open it, do I? It blows up and someone is left cleaning up a mess.

While Lilly wasn't communicating about her stresses, I was walking on eggshells, which built up stress in me. Often times when I talked to her about things that were happening with me or were bothering me, it seemed as if she either didn't care or she made it very clear that what I was saying was stupid.

Keep in mind that I said, "It seemed." As we already discussed, Aspies aren't always the best at picking up on facial cues or social things, so I can't say for sure that she didn't care or thought what I was saying was stupid, but it seemed that way to me.

If I tried to talk further and get clarification (something that is utterly crucial in an Aspie relationship) she would generally get frustrated that I didn't understand or "get it the first time." This made me shut down for long periods of time, afraid to even speak because I knew it would just end up in an argument. Anyone who knows me well will tell you that I generally never keep my mouth shut for long periods of time. Or short periods of time, for that matter!

The bottom line is that we talked a great game. To use a hockey coaching analogy, we drew up a flawless game plan before the game, but once we hit the ice, everything went out the door—including Lilly, shortly after Thanksgiving. We made a couple comeback attempts, but within a few days we were right back where we were when we initially broke up and finally decided that future attempts were futile because there was just no compatibility with communication.

So, what do Aspies need when it comes to communication? One idea is to have you each compile a list of your triggers or things that tend to set you off. Once you each have that list, put the gadgets away, turn off the TV and have a very honest conversation about each and every one of the items on both lists. Aspies, keep in mind that while your triggers can send you into meltdown mode (more on that soon), your partner's list is every bit as important as yours.

DO NOT play the "poor Aspie" card. Yes, they'll have to make some compromises and sacrifices for you based on your condition and triggers, but if you think you're getting off without making sacrifices for them, you're wrong. Give and take means just what it sounds like!

Relationships aren't a one-way street. Never forget that. A relationship isn't someone else catering to your needs while you sit back and ignore theirs. That's called being selfish and taking advantage of someone and that's the exact opposite of a relationship. A relationship is give-and-take. Not take-and-take.

If that's the kind of relationship you're currently in and your partner isn't willing to change, now is the time to hit the road. Well, not exactly at this moment. At least finish this chapter before you pack your bags and leave.

Two of my big triggers—or things that set me off—are punctuality and a lack of communication. When I say lack of communication, I don't mean that I need to know your every move. I mean that when we have plans (or are making plans), let's talk about it and figure out what's going to happen *and when*. If something needs to change with the plan, let me know as soon as possible to give me time to process it. That's what I need. In a future book on making the workplace Asperger's friendly, I'll talk a lot about this.

Aspies are notorious for needing a routine and while I learned to deal with lack of routine to a degree during the first forty-five years of my life (pre-diagnosis), routines have always been important to me. It is a trait that's driven many an NT girlfriend of mine crazy.

Sure, there are moments for spontaneity, but if we can make plans, why not do so? It makes life easier for the Aspie and ultimately for the couple, because the Aspie is more comfortable knowing what the plan is.

Enough about me. Let's get back to the meat of this chapter.

Every book you read on dating, and the overwhelming majority of them don't have anything to do with our special needs and concerns, talk about the value of communication. If communication is vital for two NT's who are dating, turn that up about twenty notches when an Aspie is involved.

Why? Well, remember that we don't always read facial cues, tone and sarcasm as well as our NT counterparts. Don't forget that our brains run on two separate frequencies and they don't always sync up with each other.

Not every Aspie / NT relationship has to be bad. There are several people I know who have very successful relationships. One person, Darrin, has been married to an NT for twenty-five years and a high school friend, Sally, is in an amazing marriage with a guy on the spectrum whom she met online.

As I mentioned before, communication is key. The couple almost has to develop their own language to communicate properly and they can't be afraid to ask for clarification if something isn't clear or if they think the other person is talking down to them. If they're truly in love, or at least in deep like, chances are that it's a misunderstanding and not the other person talking smack to their partner.

I remember one particular woman I dated and she was constantly frustrated at me for not picking up on the "signs" she was giving me. This was before I was diagnosed with Asperger's, so I had no clue why I wasn't recognizing the "signs"!

I was frustrated with myself because I couldn't pick up on her facial cues and couldn't understand why. She was upset that I wasn't picking up on the cues. In short, it was simply a bad situation all around and one that, in a situation where the Aspie has been diagnosed, can be avoided by simply sitting down and talking about things.

The NT doesn't have to stop giving facial cues. They simply need to convey the cues to their partner and then make sure their partner understands the need at hand. Yeah, it may seem weird for the two of you to be sitting at the kitchen table and the NT making faces and gestures and having the Aspie guess what the message is (kind of like facial flash cards) but the extra effort is absolutely worth it in the long run. Plus, it gives you something to laugh about down the road.

If there's no real communication in the relationship, and I say "real" because there can be surface communication without any real depth, then one partner will end up being the dominant one while the other feels stepped on.

It can go either way depending on the dynamic of the relationship. The NT could be the dominant one or the Aspie could feel in control of the situation and try to project their needs and wants over the NT and not take the partner into consideration.

If you think about this dynamic at its most basic level, it's cruel. It's one person grabbing hold of the reins and controlling the relationship. The true definition of a good relationship is an equal partnership and if one person has control of it, the dynamic becomes a dictatorship and not a partnership.

Too often in a relationship between someone on the spectrum and someone who is not, I find that the individuals begin telling themselves (usually not aloud) that their way of thinking is the best way. As Stuart Smalley from *Saturday Night Live* used to say, "That's just stinkin' thinkin'."

It drives me up the wall when I hear from others in an Aspie/NT relationship, "They don't get why I'm right and they're wrong." Guess what buddy, maybe you're not 100% right and maybe they're not 100% wrong. And if they are, maybe the problem is that you're not communicating it clearly and just trying to shove your way of doing things down their throat.

Have patience and don't be so quick to anger and frustration. That sounds very Zen, but I grew up in LA and lived there during the Phil Jackson Laker's era, so I learned things from the Zenmaster. If you try to communicate a feeling, thought or idea to your partner and they don't understand, take a breath (and maybe a sip of herbal tea) and try again. If they still don't understand, politely ask them to explain to you what they think you're saying, allow them to prove their point, and go from there.

You might need a break for a few minutes to go and process the information in your brain, be it Aspie or NT, and find another approach to the explanation. If the relationship is worth keeping, it's worth the few minutes it takes to formulate an explanation that your partner understands.

This is how you develop, what I call, your own special language. It may not and probably will not be a traditional language, but over time you'll learn what words and phrases work and what your partner does and doesn't understand. As you learn these things, file them away and use them over and over so as to simplify your communication. The happiest couples I know who are in stable Aspie/NT relationships, some as long as twenty-five years, have done this.

The Bible talks about a love language, but this is a different type of love language. It's a special language you and your partner come up with over time because you love each other and want to communicate properly rather than by yelling, screaming and throwing things. No one needs the cops being called when, with a little time and slightly more patience, you can create a language that saves both your relationship and bail money.

You've heard the phrase, "Laughter is the best medicine," right? Well, it's true and I think especially true in the Aspie/NT relationship. Probably more so than in a traditional NT/NT relationship. There will be moments of embarrassment for both of you and if you can't find a way to laugh about it (now and not down the road) then life may get pretty rocky.

Look, we all do and say stupid things that can be laughed about. Ask anyone who's known me for a while and they'll tell you that I'm the king of saying the wrong thing at the wrong time and for a lot of years, even after my diagnosis of Asperger's, I couldn't laugh at those moments.

Instead, I replayed them over and over in my head, beating myself up for being such a moron, but that got me nowhere except constantly in a bad mood and my self-esteem was in the toilet because I was just waiting for the next stupid thing to come out of my mouth. I still wait for the next stupid thing to come out of my mouth, but now I can generally laugh about them.

When you, as a couple have those moments, be prepared to laugh them off and move forward. If you don't, I can tell you from experience, those moments have the power to kill an entire weekend as the person who put their foot in their mouth stews over the moment and won't let it go.

NT's, remember that your Aspie partner sometimes has a problem with showing their feelings and it's hard for us to navigate the waters of the social world and sometimes we appear insensitive. If you know, or at least believe that you're in a solid relationship and you feel your partner has been—or is being—insensitive to you, this is a great time for some communication and questions. *Just make sure the questions don't come off as an interrogation.*

"You just said _____ and that hurt my feelings. I don't think you meant to. Can you please explain what you meant by that?" Is much better than, "What the hell did you mean by that?"

Also, remember that the Aspie can get overwhelmed by their triggers and need some time alone to let the moment pass. When (not if) that happens, the NT has to be willing to put the pending discussion on the back burner for a bit and give the Aspie their space so we can get our heads back on straight and can come back ready to talk and figure out whatever it is that needs to get worked out between us.

As a person who just wants to get things done, I can tell you from experience that it's not an easy task to let your partner have their space for a while, because we just want to get the situation over with and put behind us. Trust me, in the long run, the time to let your partner process and get mentally and emotionally ready to communicate is worth it.

Also, it's not always the Aspie who needs some time and space to process things. NT's also have that need and as Aspie's we need to understand and recognize that. If they're willing to do that for us, then we have to be willing to do it for them. After all, fair is fair.

Giving one another space and time is called respect and, ironically enough, RESPECT is the subject of the next chapter. Let's forge ahead with a discussion on respect.

Ch. 5 R.E.S.P.E.C.T.

Every time I head the word "respect" I'm sad to admit that I think of the TV show *Always Sunny in Philadelphia*. It is definitely NOT everyone's cup of tea, but in one episode, Mac, Charlie and Frank are talking about respect and they say that respect is number one and it's the name of almost every game.

It's definitely the name of the dating-and-relationship game and before we speak or act, we need to think about what our words and actions are going to do to our partner both mentally and emotionally.

I don't mean that we'll necessarily scar them for life by one of our actions, although depending on the severity of what we do, that is a definite possibility.

Let's assume, though, that we're not talking about a life-or-death situation but rather a regular disagreement. A great example, using me, is that when I feel disrespected or that someone is talking down to me, it pulls me off my game and I have to pull away from whatever I'm doing in order to get my head on straight so I can get back to it, focus and give it one hundred percent.

If you want to know the honest truth, it's happened several times as I've been writing this book. Something happens, usually not on purpose by someone, and it throws me off my game. When it comes to writing, I'm a go-big-or-go-home kind of guy and if I know I can't write at the top of my game, I don't want to put out garbage I'll have to re-write later. To me it seems like a huge waste of my time.

Since I'm not in a relationship or dating anyone at the moment, these disrespectful moments are coming from elsewhere, but I think you get the point of what I'm saying.

I'm not discounting the NT in the relationship as their feelings are every bit as important as those of the Aspie, but sometimes the littlest things throw us into the biggest funk. So I'm asking the NT's to please watch not only what you say, but also how you say things to your partner on the spectrum. It can avoid problems and make for a much better day, week and weekend.

That being said, Aspies, you don't get a free pass. Think before you speak and if you get even the slightest notion that you've somehow offended your partner, quickly ask how you've offended them so you can clarify. NT's, keeping in mind that we don't always pick up on those cues, so if you feel disrespected, immediately tell your partner how and why you feel that way and ask them to explain further what they meant.

If they can find a way to clarify and make it clear that no disrespect was intended, great. If not, then I leave it to you both to work out the situation as you see fit, keeping in mind that violence never solves anything.

I vividly remember one encounter where a woman I was dating felt highly disrespected by something I did though I felt totally innocent. It didn't matter how many times I explained myself, it didn't get any better. This was before my diagnosis, so I had nothing to back myself up. I was just stuck, trying to keep my head above water.

We had been dating for quite a while and had just spent time being intimate. Afterwards, she went to take a shower and I went into the kitchen. Suddenly I remembered that she was going to pick up buy tickets for an event and that I was supposed to give her $50 to get them.

While she was in the shower I walked back into my bedroom, saw her purse on the nightstand and laid $50 next to her purse. A short time later, a very angry towel-clad woman stormed into the kitchen clutching the money and screaming, "Is this what you think of me now?"

"What?" I asked, not at all sure what was going on.

"Do you think you have to pay me for services rendered and do you think I'm really only worth $50?"

"No," I said, "Remember the tickets you're getting? I thought about it and while I was thinking about it, I put the money by your purse so I wouldn't forget it later."

She wasn't buying it and for the next half hour I got a very loud lecture on respect and how I could have handed her the money at a later time. I kept explaining that while it was on my mind I wanted to take care of it and that I meant absolutely no disrespect and that she shouldn't be taking it that way.

She went back to the bedroom to get changed, but several hours later she was still on the same topic and still berating me, so I simply asked for the $50 back, asked her to leave and never come back. Please don't think I'm insensitive for dumping someone over this issue. Call it the straw that broke the camel's back.

This is a great example of an Aspie trying to do the right thing and the NT partner taking it the wrong way and not communicating about the problem at hand. Yelling at your partner and not listening to anything they say is neither communication nor respect and without either, you don't have a strong foundation for a relationship.

Respect isn't something that only happens in the home or when the two of you are alone. It happens in public as well and is made evident by the way you treat one another in front of your friends, family, coworkers and complete strangers.

Just as two Neurotypicals dating are expected to show each other respect, the same goes for the Aspie/NT pairing. The NT needs to be respectful of the fact that the Aspie may have some triggers that limit what they can do as a couple, but the Aspie also needs to be respectful of the NT and remember that they aren't there to completely shut off their social life.

If the NT is into skydiving and the Aspie is terrified of heights, then they should kiss their partner goodbye as they head out the door to go skydiving with their friends. Respecting the things that your partner likes and you don't can go a long way towards building a healthy relationship

Compromises have to be made in relationships, especially in relationships where there are limitations due to one partner being on the spectrum. That being said, the Aspie can, with the help of the NT, try some things that normally would trigger them and see if they can find a way to make things work. Maybe it will and maybe it won't, but some things are worth trying.

For example, there's a local TV show that tapes three episodes once a month. The theatre is about forty-five minutes from my house and holds about seven hundred people. Being in crowds like that, even with my service dog, terrifies me. I spent quite a bit of time thinking about how I could go to the show and not have a panic attack and I finally came up with a plan:

I got to the theatre early, before most of the crowd showed up, and immediately found a seat on the aisle in the back row of the balcony, the least crowded part of the theatre. That alone cut down the number of people I was around and by getting there early and planting myself in my seat, I avoided seeing most of the crowd.

When the third episode was nearly over, I quietly slipped out the door, through the lobby and onto the street, thus avoiding the seven hundred people who would be pouring out behind me and freaking me out beyond belief. By taking the time to devise a plan and try it out, I was able to find a way to do something I normally wouldn't be able to do.

I figured the worst that could happen is that I would get into the crowded room and start feeling panicky and simply bail. Doing that would only put me out the $10 I paid for the taping and a portion of that money was going to charity anyway, so either way I wouldn't feel too bad about my experiment.

We're almost finished so let's push on to the rest of the principles.

Ch. 6 Everything Else

So far we've discussed communication and respect. That leaves us with understanding, honesty and sharing. If you really think about it, if you're communicating properly and respecting one another, chances are pretty good that you're already understanding, being honest and sharing. But let's talk about them a bit anyway.

A lot of times I hear people say that they understand what their partner's limitations are or what their partner has to go through in order to make a relationship with them work, but do they really? I think a lot of us say we understand, but what I want to know is this: Do you truly get what it's like for your partner?

If you were asked to walk in their shoes or to describe what your partner goes through—mentally, emotionally and physically—in a typical day, could you articulate that? If the answer is no, then you don't truly understand your partner.

Don't get down on yourself for answering no, because I believe this is something that comes with time together, communicating feelings and experiences. That's why I listed communication first, because communication is the cornerstone of the whole relationship. You have to be able to communicate and be best friends for an Aspie and NT relationship to grow and thrive. This is not something that happens overnight.

Sure, the communication may start right away and might be amazing and you could start laying a solid foundation for the rest of your life from date one, but it's going to take time before you see that solid structure form.

I'm not getting Biblical on you with this analogy, because that's what it is—an analogy that Christians, Muslims, Buddhists, atheists, agnostics, and anyone else, can understand.

It's like the parable of the man who builds his house on the sand and the man who builds his house on the rock, or a solid surface. If you want your relationship to last and to be solid, you have to build it on a solid surface and that solid surface begins with the principles of communication, respect, honesty, understanding, sharing, and ultimately, love.

If you decide to build your relationship on a shaky surface like sand, or in this case, deception, hiding things, not talking, etc., when the first big storm hits, there goes your relationship.

Both the Aspie and the NT have to understand each other and, admittedly, that takes time. It's important, however, to begin that process of understanding early on so that you're both on the same page and that you know what you're really getting into. Not every NT is ready to jump into a relationship with someone on the spectrum and if that's you, there's nothing to be ashamed about. It's the way you are and no one is asking you to change who you are. If you have to change yourself, it's definitely NOT the right relationship for you.

Likewise, not every Aspie is ready for a relationship with someone off the spectrum. We may find them confusing, unclear and, at first, hard to trust. That's why honesty and trust are so important.

Remember earlier when we talked about the Aspie not always being able to recognize sarcasm and facial cues? The same goes for our partner or potential partner. If the Aspie doesn't trust that you have their back and that you'll look out for them and be there for them, there will be zero chance of a healthy relationship.

I'm not putting this all on the NT, not at all. Relationships are a fifty-fifty deal. I'm just saying that at first the NT has to make sure the Aspie realizes you care for them on some level (let's face it, falling in love at first sight is more of a storybook thing than a non-fiction thing).

If they don't believe that you care about them, it will be hard for them to trust you and without trust, the house you two are building is starting off on that sandy foundation and not the solid foundation that it needs to survive the storms ahead.

Now, while the NT is making sure the Aspie understands they are cared about, the Aspie needs to come clean about their triggers, fears and other things that set them apart and make them unique. These things need to get talked about early for a couple reasons.

First, it's not fair to hide things from your partner. Remember that honesty is one of the key principles in the Aspie/NT relationship. The NT has to be aware early on what they're getting into and what they're going to deal with on a regular basis.

Playing games and hiding who you really are is bad in any type of relationship, but for someone on the spectrum—who comes with a special set of circumstances—it's crucial. You don't need to break out everything on the first date, but after two or three dates, when it appears that things may be starting to get serious, you two should probably sit down over a drink (if you indulge in alcohol) and depending on what you have to share, maybe keep the bottle handy. Since moving from California to the Ozarks, my go-to is blackberry moonshine and 7 Up, but coffee or tea will work just fine if you don't imbibe in liquor.

FYI, I'm kidding about needing to drink as you share your Aspie self with your potential partner. Why? Because there's absolutely nothing to be ashamed about. Unlike one national organization that thinks people on the spectrum need to be cured, we don't need to be cured and if we can't share both the good and bad about ourselves with the other person, it's probably not the right person for us.

Don't worry Aspies, because at this share session, you won't be the only one getting things off your chest. This is the time for the NT to share their feelings, quirks, traits and what they need as well as what they absolutely don't want in a partner.

Now you two are doing some serious conversing and getting real with each other. It may feel weird at first, but I assure you that it's the right thing to do and if the relationship is right, this is the time where you will both realize it and start to figure out how to make things work between the two of you. Granted, you'll continue to learn things over time and fine-tune the relationship, but this first major conversation is where it all starts.

The other reason it's important to share these things early on is, as mentioned before, if one of you can't handle something that's a deal breaker for the other, it's better to know sooner rather than later when feelings are deeper and you're more likely to feel deep emotional pain.

Remember how Aspies are prone to depression? Think back to your last breakup and how you felt after that. It probably wasn't great was it? Maybe it was. If it was, think back to the last breakup where you were really hurting afterwards. The longer you wait to be honest with your dating partner and truly begin to understand one another other, the worse the pain will be if things have to end. I don't want to see anyone in pain, especially when it can be avoided simply by having a conversation early on.

Understanding each other is a process that starts on day one and doesn't end until the relationship does. Both the Aspie and the NT will regularly learn things about their partner and what makes them tick. It may be observing a morning routine and one day having the light bulb go on as to why a certain part of that routine is so important, or someone using a phrase and having the partner say they don't like that phrase because it reminds them of an old boyfriend/girlfriend.

The point is that as the love grows, so does the understanding. Or is it as the understanding grows, so does the love? I guess they go hand in hand. The more you understand your partner, the more you love them and the more you love them, the more you understand them.

In order to understand your partner, you inevitably have to ask questions. Just make sure you don't do it in a way that makes your partner feel like they're being interrogated or grilled and definitely don't shine a bright light in their face as you're asking questions. That's so '70s cop show.

Here's a pretty extreme example, but one that I'm sure happens all the time, and it's a conversation that I'm sure starts out wrong and ends even worse. Yes, I'm talking about watching porn.

Ladies, don't even try to pretend that you're totally innocent when it comes to this. While I'm very sure that men are guilty of this more than women, I know for a fact that plenty of women have been known to visit sites that, shall we say, can't be viewed in schools, libraries or other public places.

After catching your partner in the act of watching porn, or after viewing a computer's browser history, one person (usually the woman) goes straight into "Bad Cop" mode. Out comes the phone book, if they even make phone books anymore, (because phone books don't leave marks) and the light shines in the guy's face. At this point it really doesn't matter which is the Aspie or the NT, because all that matters is that she (usually) is all kinds of upset.

Here's my first tip towards communication and understanding in this situation. Do NOT start the questioning by asking "What the hell?" or "Am I not hot enough for you? Is that it?"

This is the time to take a moment, catch your breath and start by asking what's going on with them and going on inside their head, Find out what the real problem is so you can start working on that. It may be as simple as two people with different sex drives—something we'll be discussing in the next couple pages when we start the final chapter (the chapter on sex).

If one partner is hiding porn from the other, there's no doubt there's a problem, but the way to solve it is through having a discussion and not starting something that you'll both walk away from feeling horrible.

Once again, this is where honesty comes in. Whoever got busted, don't make excuses, dance around the subject or try to play it off like it's no big deal. If your partner is confronting you about it, it is a big deal to them. Be an adult and own it. You don't have to be proud of it, but own up to it and then, and only then, can you have a truly meaningful conversation and get to the root of why it happened.

A final word to the busted party, you should never BS your partner and you should always be honest with them. If there was ever a time to NOT lie to them, this is THAT time. Be straight. Be honest. Work out the problems like adults without raising voices, bringing up past indiscretions of the other party, and by all means NEVER bring up someone's family member in a fight, especially a fight of this nature.

These are the moments, in the heat of battle, where we are most likely to forget everything we read and learned in this book, but it's also the time when we need to remember the principles the most.

That being said, let's move onto the final chapter, the chapter on sex.

Ch.7 Yes. The "S" Word

It's something most of us think about a regular basis, some of us on too-regular a basis. It's something we generally enjoy doing though some far more than others and though we enjoy the act, we rarely enjoy talking about it.

Yes. I'm talking about sex.

Sex is a healthy part of adult relationship and marriage, and those with Asperger's often times have sex drives that are higher than their NT partners. Or, they have virtually no sex drive. There seems to be no middle ground when it comes to the sex drive of an Aspie.

One thing I learned as I was doing research for this book, and something that amazed me, is that a number of people on the spectrum are into very kinky sex. I thought that was a bit strange, until I heard the explanation, and then it made perfect sense.

In kinky sex there are rules and regulations. There are safe words and lines you simply don't cross without express verbal permission. Seeing as how Aspies thrive on rules, routine and stability, it makes perfect sense that some of us would take our proclivities in this direction.

I personally think that in adult interactions where both partners are open to having a sexual relationship, a discussion should be had regarding sex drives, needs, wants and things of that nature. In an Aspie/NT relationship it is absolutely crucial that this conversation take place sooner rather than later.

In fact, I believe the conversation should be part of the large conversation discussed in the last chapter. That doesn't mean that sex has to start happening right away. Every couple takes things at their own pace and knows when it's right for them, but sex with someone on the spectrum can bring it's own unique set of challenges.

For example, as mentioned numerous times throughout this book, routine is important to us, so some (not all) Aspies will get into a routine with their partner and not want to deviate from it. They will want to start the same way, with "A" and then move on to "B", then "C" and so on.

But wait. Maybe it's not the Aspie who craves a routine. Maybe the NT has a need or desire for familiarity and the Aspie is all too willing to try new things. This is why the conversation is so important; to see if you're on the same page, and if not, how you can make this work in a way that will leave you both happy and satisfied.

That's the key to all this, that at the end of it, you're both left feeling happy and satisfied and not having one of you feeling as though you gave in to your partner's desires and "did it their way to make them happy."

Does one of you crave routine? Discuss it and see just how big a deal routine is and if other, uh, variables, can be introduced. I mean, unless you've tried it, you don't know if you like it, right? Keep in mind, that principle does NOT apply to all things sexual!

Find out if your partner is willing to throw a new position into the routine and see how it goes. Who knows? He or she may like it. If not, then go back to the drawing board. Or maybe, instead of going, A, B, C, D, once in a while try B, D, A, C.

When it comes to sex, conversation can be very uncomfortable and I can't count the number of conversations I've had (note I didn't say the number of partners I've had) who think I'm crazy for wanting to talk about sex. I'm sorry but I'm full-blown Aspie and while I'm not one of those who has to go in a certain routine, I do like to talk about wants, likes, needs, things that are off limits, things that bring up bad memories of past partners, and so on.

Why have these types of conversations? Because I can tell you from experience that nothing kills a mood quicker than trying something and getting pushed away because your partner either flat-out doesn't like it or because their old boyfriend did that and it's a bad reminder.

As the relationship grows, the emotional intimacy should become just as amazing as the physical and if there are no conversations ahead of time, one move can kill the emotional connection in one partner, and not just for the night. Or day.

These conversations can be difficult to be sure, but think about your life up to this point. Haven't some of the toughest conversations you've ever had turned out to be some of the best in terms of the results?

The same applies here. If you want to have a long, awesome relationship with your partner, a great sex life should be part of that equation. I'm not saying that you should want to jump each other every day (although that may work for some couples). What I'm saying is that when you do become intimate with your partner, it should be amazing and satisfying and you should see fireworks, unicorns and all sorts of crazy, amazing things in your head. And your partner should as well.

The bottom line is that in order to have an amazing, satisfying sex life, all five principles we've discussed in this book come into play. There definitely needs to be communication, both before, during, and after. There definitely needs to be respect. We're not degrading our partner, we're showing them we care, even if that involves a bit of kink—if that's your thing.

It definitely involves honesty, as both partners need to be upfront about likes, dislikes and desires. Also, women, don't fake orgasms. As a guy, I can say that we hate that. If it didn't happen, it didn't happen. Let us find a way to satisfy you without you pretending! Finally there's sharing. You two are sharing your bodies, your emotions and your hearts with one another and that is a beautiful thing.

Conclusion

As someone who is fifty-two and was diagnosed with Asperger's at the age of forty-six, I like to say that I grew up off the spectrum. This means that every relationship I've been in has been an Aspie/NT relationship only I didn't know it for most of my life. Because of this lack of diagnosis and lack of knowledge, the relationships have been pretty bad and I learned a lot. That's where the idea for this book came from. So that you wouldn't have to go through the same things I went through and endure the nasty comments and harsh ridicule from women who thought I was weird (and a few other colorful words which I choose not to mention). Dating, marriage and relationships are always a learning experience and my hope is that because of this book, you learn something about yourself and how to have a great relationship with the person who is right for you.

Thank you for buying and reading this book. I kept it short, sweet and simple because I think these principles are enough to get you going. Every couple is different and with this foundation I'm confident you'll find what works best for you.

If you bought this on Amazon or Kindle and you enjoyed it, please leave a review. It will help me immensely. If you bought it at www.purplechin.com or elsewhere, please feel free to use the contact form on the Purple Chin website and let me know what you thought.

In the next few months I will be releasing two more titles, both of which will be available at the same place you purchased this one. *An Asperger's Guide To Navigating the Workplace* will help my fellow Aspies thrive in an environment that generally terrifies us the most. I bet you didn't know that 85% of high-functioning autistics don't hold down jobs because their fear and lack of social skills don't allow them to get through the job interview. This book will help that.

Asperger's Isn't Contagious: Helping High School & College Students Understand and Include Their Autistic Peers In Social Groups, is exactly as it sounds. It's a guide for NT's to help understand us and include us so we don't feel alone and friendless.

As an Adult Asperger's advocate I'm available to speak to groups from high school age on up and if you would like me to come speak to your group, please use the contact form at www.purplechin.com

Again, thank you so much for investing not only your money, but also your time in this book. I'm sure that if you work hard and apply these principles, you'll have an amazing relationship for a very long time!

Made in the USA
Monee, IL
29 March 2021